中 国 话 听 力

Chinese Through Listening

1

中 国 话 语 音 基 础

Rudiments of Chinese
Phonetics

FOREIGN LANGUAGES PRESS
BEIJING

First Edition   1983

ISBN 0-8351-1183-0

Published by the Foreign Languages Press
24 Baiwanzhuang Road, Beijing, China

Printed by the Foreign Languages Printing House
19 West Chegongzhuang Road, Beijing, China

Distributed by China Publications Centre (Guoji Shudian)
P.O. Box 399, Beijing, China

Printed in the People's Republic of China

《中 国 话 听 力》
说　　明

（一）对象

《中国话听力》（包括磁带及使用说明）的主要使用者是在世界各地学习中国话但缺乏语言环境的人们。它针对初学者、中级水平或较高水平的进修者的不同情况，由浅入深地提供一套完整的听力训练材料，可供自学，也可供教学辅导。这一套磁带联成一个整体，但各盘又是相对独立的，可以根据学习者的不同程度和要求，分别选用。

（二）目标

编制这套听力材料的总原则是：以语言信息理论为指导，针对外国人学中国话的听力困难，结合中国人日常生活的语言实践，根据中国话本身的特点，在语音接收和语义理解两方面提供全新的训练方法。它的目标是通过这一套材料，帮助学习者获得听懂中国话的基本技能。

（三）内容

《中国话听力》包括：

A．初级部分

中国话语音基础

中国话听力入门

B. 中级部分

  在北京生活

  在中国旅行

C. 高级部分

  广播、课堂

  中国文化欣赏

（以上各专题都有标准录音磁带及使用文字说明。）

此外，跟它配套的还有一本《中国话听力的理论和实践》以及一本《中国话听力词汇手册》，可供使用者参考。

这一套《中国话听力》由王力教授、周有光教授担任审订工作，由吴宗济教授担任语音指导，由申葆青副教授担任英语翻译。

《中国话语音基础》磁带发音人是刘骥和郝洁平，英语解说是申葆青，由赵平担任录音剪辑工作。感谢 Harvey Taylor 先生和 Marcia Bliss Marks 女士对于英译文提出宝贵意见。

编　者　陈明远

朱　竹

刘　骥

1982 年 6 月

CHINESE THROUGH LISTENING
EXPLANATORY NOTES

1. For whom the course is intended

Chinese Through Listening is a course intended for those who are learning to speak Chinese in a non-Chinese environment. It comprises three units, ranging from easy to difficult, catering respectively to learners at the elementary, the intermediate and the advanced level. All the lessons are recorded on cassette tapes with corresponding scripts and directions on how to use them. This set of tapes is an integrated whole, but relative independence has been allowed for each individual unit. Thus learners at different levels can study just what is most needed from any of the three stages. It can be used for self-study or as a supplement to classroom study.

2. Aims

The general principle underlying the compilation of the aural comprehension materials is the treating of language as a set of signals. This provides for an entirely new approach: the training of the hearer to receive sound signals and to understand their semantic meanings. Special difficulties in aural comprehension arising from learning Chinese as a foreign language and peculiarities of the Chinese language are also taken into account. The language style used in the materials is the Putonghua (Standard Chinese) which people in China speak every day. The entire course is aimed at helping the learners to acquire the basic skills needed for understanding spoken Chinese.

3. Contents

Unit A   Elementary Level

        1) Rudiments of Chinese Phonetics
        2) Elementary Aural Comprehension

Unit B   Intermediate Level

        1) Living in Beijing
        2) Travelling in China

Unit C   Advanced Level

        1) Broadcasts and Lectures
        2) Appreciating Chinese Culture

(For each of the topics listed above, there is a cassette tape with printed directions on how to use it.)

Besides, for reference of learners using the tapes, two more booklets are available: *The Theory and Practice of Chinese Through Listening* and *A Glossary for Chinese Through Listening*

The examiners of *Chinese Through Listening* are Professor Wang Li and Professor Zhou Youguang, with Professor Wu Zongji as advisor in phonetics and Associate Professor Shen Baoqing as translator.

Special thanks go to Dr. Harvey Taylor and Miss Marcia Bliss Marks for the advice and comments on the English translation.

Compilers: Chén Míngyuǎn
              Zhū Zhú
              Liú Jì

June 1982

《中国话听力》序

王力

《中国话听力》共六分册，配有录音磁带和文字说明，供外国人学习中国语使用。在我国，是首次向世界各地正式发行这样一套听力材料。

它的特点是：力求把我国现代语言学的理论研究成果和语音实验数据，跟中国话作为外语的教学实践，有机地结合起来。例如在语音部分，对于声母、韵母、基本音节及音节组合的教学方法，都作了新的安排。在听力的四阶段的训练过程里，突出了中国话本身的特点，强调区别易混的成分，注重识别语流里的标记，等等。在这套听力材料中，展现了同中国话进行交际的各种情景：在北京的日常生活、在中国各地的旅行、中国的广播和课堂、中国文化的欣赏。通过这些生动的情景，由浅入深地、系统地培养外国人听懂中国话的能力。在语音信息的接收和理解上，它尝试采取一些新的训练方式。今后还将根据实际经验，不断加以修订，以臻完善。

中国话有三千多年的文字记载。全世界有五分之一以上的人口使用中国话。在历史发展的悠久性和地理分布的广泛性这两方面，中国话是首屈一指的。虽然繁难的方块汉字使中国的书面语言成为一门艰深的学问，但是中国话作为口语，则是比较容易掌握的。特别是在这一套《中国语听力》文字材料中，始终采用汉语拼音作为学习中国话的工具。由于拼写法跟实际读音完全一致，就更便于外国人学习了。

希望这一套《中国话听力》在帮助外国人学习中国话的过程中获得成功。

1983年1月10日

FOREWORD

"Chinese Through Listening" consists of six volumes of text with accompanying cassette tapes designed to aid foreign students in learning spoken Chinese. It is the first such aid published in China for distribution abroad.

A special feature of this course is that it aims to integrate effectively the results of theoretical research in modern Chinese linguistics and the data gained in phonetic experiments with practical experience in teaching Chinese as a foreign language. In phonetics, for instance, a new approach has been introduced in the teaching of the initials, the finals, the basic syllables and syllable combinations. Throughout all the four stages in training listening comprehension, special attention has been focused on the characteristics of the spoken word of the Chinese language, emphasizing the differences between those elements which are easily confused and laying stress on recognizing the markers in connected speech.

This set of listening comprehension material presents various situations in which spoken Chinese is used for communication: everyday life in Beijing, a tour of different parts of China, broadcasts and lectures in China and appreciation of Chinese culture. Through these lively situations the foreign students are trained to understand spoken Chinese from simple to more and more complex sentences. New methods of training are adopted to help the students receive

1

and comprehend phonetic information. Further revisions and improvements based on teaching experience will be made so as to bring this material closer to perfection.

The Chinese language has a written record of more than 3,000 years. It is spoken by over one-fifth of the world's population. It has no equal in length of historical development and scope of geographical distribution. Although the complicated Chinese characters make the mastery of writing Chinese a difficult academic endeavor, oral Chinese is relatively easy to learn. It is more so since the Pinyin spelling is used all through the written text of this set of *"Chinese Through Listening"* as a tool for learning spoken Chinese. The foreign student will find it much easier to learn since this spelling system closely represents the actual pronunciation.

It is our hope that this set of *"Chinese Through Listening"* will be a success in helping foreign students learn spoken Chinese.

Wang Li
January 10, 1983

CONTENTS

RUDIMENTS OF CHINESE PHONETICS

Rudiments of Chinese Phonetics, the first part of *Chinese Through Listening*, teaches you correct Chinese pronunciation and acquaints you with the 404 basic syllables in the Chinese language. The exercises on the 110 syllables in common use and intensive drills on the combination of tones are intended to help you learn and distinguish the four tones.

If you have learned to say the four tones the way a native speaker says them by the time you finish this part, it means you are ready to move on to the next part which teaches you the basics of understanding spoken Chinese.

I. THE CHINESE PHONETIC ALPHABET
(Hanyu Pinyin)

△name:	Aa	Bb	Cc	Dd	Ee	Ff	Gg
	a	bê	cê	dê	e	êf	gê
	Hh	Ii	Jj	Kk	Ll	Mm	Nn
	ha	i	jie	kê	êl	êm	nê
	Oo	Pp	Qq	Rr	Ss	Tt	
	o	pê	qiu	ar	ês	tê	
	Uu	Vv	Ww	Xx	Yy	Zz	
	u	vê	wa	xi	ya	zê△ *	

*The paragraphs between two △ are recorded on the tape.

5

II. INITIALS

△The Chinese syllable is usually composed of an initial and a final, and each syllable has four different tones. The initial is a consonant that begins the syllable and the final is the rest of the syllable, e.g. "bang" in which "b" is an initial and "ang" is a final.

There are 23 initials in Chinese:

b	[b̥]	p	[p']	m	[m]	f	[f]	w	[w]
d	[d̥]	t	[t']	n	[n]	l	[l]		
g	[g̊]	k	[k']			h	[x]		
z	[d̥s]	c	[ts']			s	[s]		
zh	[d̥ʂ]	ch	[tʂ']			sh	[ʂ]	r	[ɹ]
j	[d̥ɕ]	q	[tɕ']			x	[ɕ]	y	[j]

Please bear this in mind: The Chinese initials are not syllabic sounds. No word in Chinese consists of only an initial.△

When you have listened through the list of Chinese initials, compare them with the consonant sounds in your own language and try to tell the difference between the two. Now, with your eyes on the list, listen to the tape once again, repeat each sound after the tape and see if you can pronounce it properly. In the following six pairs of initials, the first one is unaspirated, the second aspirated: b—p, d—t, g—k, j—q, z—c and zh—ch. You may find it difficult to make an aspirated sound and you may confuse it with an unaspirated one, but there is a way to tell the difference: hold a thin piece of paper before your mouth and see whether it is pushed by the air coming out of your mouth when you are making the sounds. The paper should not stir when the sounds b, d, g, j, z, zh are made. But it should, when p, t, k, q, c, ch are pronounced. You can easily tell the difference in this way.

There are three more pairs of initials: zh—z, ch—c and sh—s. The first one, a retroflex one, is made by curling the tip of the tongue a bit towards the hard palate, the second is made without curling the tongue. If your zh, ch and sh do not sound right, it may be because you fail to curl the tip of your tongue in pronouncing them. So try again and curl the tip of your tongue.

III. FINALS

△There are 36 finals in Chinese:

a	[A]	o	[o]	e	[ɤ]	ɿ	[ɿ,ʅ]	er	[ɚ]
		ai	[ai]	ei	[ei]	ao	[au]	ou	[əu]
		an	[an]	en	[ən]	ang	[aŋ]	eng	[əŋ]
i	[i]	ia	[iA]	ie	[iɛ]	iao	[iau]	iu	[iəu]
		ian	[iɛn]	in	[in]	iang	[iaŋ]	ing	[iŋ]
u	[u]	ua	[uA]	uo	[uɔ]	uai	[uai]	ui	[uei]
		uan	[uan]	un	[uən]	uang	[uaŋ]	ong	[oŋ]
ü	[y]	üe	[yɛ]	üan	[yan]	ün	[yn]	iong	[yoŋ]

You may have noticed that most of the finals in the Chinese Phonetic Alphabet are combinations of more than one vowel sound instead of a single vowel sound.△

7

A final in Chinese is a vowel, which may be a simple vowel (simple final) or a compound vowel (compound final), or a vowel plus a nasal consonant (nasal final). Some syllables may be without an initial, e.g. "a" (a modal particle), but no syllable can do without a final.

△We advise you to follow the same procedure of listening and repeating after the tape in learning the finals.△

IV. BASIC SYLLABLES

△Some people say Chinese is a difficult language, but it is not quite so difficult as they think.

There are 404 basic syllables in Chinese. We have worked out a "Table of Chinese Basic Syllables" that gives you a bird's-eye view of all the 404 syllables. Now listen to the syllables in this table as you follow with your eyes.△ (See Table of Chinese Basic Syllables.)

△All the syllables were read using the first tone. Of course, there will be more than 404 sounds if each one is read with all its different tones.△

In the "Table of Chinese Basic Syllables" you find finals in the top row and initials in the left column. Combine an initial and a final and you form a basic syllable. Repeat after the tape while listening. You will need to practise over and over again those syllables that you find most difficult to pronounce.

V. TONES

When a syllable of Chinese is pronounced in different tones, it has different meanings, e.g. dā (to put up), dá (to answer), dǎ (to beat), dà (big, large); tāng (soup), táng (sugar), tǎng (to lie), tàng (to scald).

△The most difficult part for a foreigner learning Chinese is, perhaps, its tones. Yet it need not be so difficult to learn them, since there are only four basic tones in Chinese. Now listen to this:

ā	á	ǎ	à
ē	é	ě	è
yōu	yóu	yǒu	yòu
wāng	wáng	wǎng	wàng
yuān	yuán	yuǎn	yuàn

Now you probably have some idea of what the four tones in Chinese are like. However, there is something more you should know: in addition to the four basic tones, there is one special and important change of tone called the neutral tone. The neutral tone is not an independent element that stands by itself; it occurs only in connection with and related to the tone preceding it. But that does not necessarily mean that this neutral tone is less important than the other four tones, since you will never be able to speak Chinese accurately and with a natural flow if you don't know where to use a neutral tone in your speech.

Now please listen to this — A neutral tone following a first, second, third or fourth tone sounds like this:

mǎma	妈妈	bōli	玻璃	tā ne	他呢
yéye	爷爷	biéde	别的	láile	来了
jiějie	姐姐	sǎngzi	嗓子	zǒu ba	走吧
xièxie	谢谢	mùtou	木头	lèi ma	累吗

Please note that the tone-mark is placed above the main vowel of the final in each syllable. For a neutral tone, no tone-mark is needed.△

For the convenience of the learner, four marks are used to stand for the four tones of a Chinese syllable. Thus, " – " stands for Tone 1, " ´ " for Tone 2, " ˇ " for Tone 3 and " ˋ " for Tone 4.

What makes Chinese so difficult for the foreign learner may be the fact that each Chinese syllable has a definite tone. Here are the main characteristics of each tone: Tone 1 is a high level pitch; Tone 2 is a rising pitch; Tone 3 is a low dipping pitch; Tone 4 is a falling pitch. When practising, please note that if there are two Tone 3 syllables in the same tone combination, the first syllable should be articulated in Tone 2 instead of Tone 3. The neutral tone is short and unstressed.

Try hard to imitate and learn the four basic tones. Your proficiency can be tested by your ability or inability to tell which tone is used as soon as you hear a word spoken.

VI. DRILLING ON INITIALS

△The beauty of the Chinese language lies not only in the music and euphony of its different tones, but also in the rhythm of its disyllabic forms. The following are some samples of disyllabic words with the same initial in both syllables. Listen to these carefully to get a better idea of what the Chinese initials are like.

bàba	爸爸	pīngpāng	乒乓	mìmì	秘密
fēngfù	丰富	wénwù	文物	děngděng	等等
tàntǎo	探讨	niúnǎi	牛奶	lǎolao	姥姥
gēge	哥哥	kěkào	可靠	hěn hǎo	很好
zuì zǎo	最早	cóngcǐ	从此	sānsuì	三岁
zhēnzhèng	真正	chéng chē	乘车	shūshu	叔叔
réngrán	仍然	jiùjiu	舅舅	qīnqi	亲戚
xuéxí	学习	yǒuyòng	有用△		

In pronouncing the following words with the same initials, pay attention to whether the initial is an aspirated or an unaspirated one, a retroflex one or not. You need to repeat after the tape at least twice.

VII. DRILLING ON FINALS

△The following are disyllabic words with the same final in both syllables. Listen to these carefully to get a better idea of what the Chinese finals are like.

dàmā	大妈	bómó	薄膜
hégé	合格	jīqì	机器
fúwù	服务	yǔjù	语句
zìsī	自私	zhǐshì	指示
báicài	白菜	Běi-Měi	北美

11

bàodǎo	报导	Ouzhōu	欧洲
gǎntàn	感叹	gēnběn	根本
āngzāng	肮脏	fēngzheng	风筝
jiǎyá	假牙	tiēqiè	贴切
xiǎoniǎo	小鸟	jiǔliú	久留
diànxiàn	电线	pīnyīn	拼音
xiǎngliàng	响亮	píngjìng	平静
huàhuār	画花儿	luōsuo	罗嗦
shuāihuài	摔坏	cuīhuǐ	摧毁
zhuǎnhuàn	转换	Kūnlún	昆仑
chuāngkuàng	窗框	gōngnóng	工农
yuēlüè	约略	yuánquán	源泉
jūnyún	均匀	xiōngyǒng	汹涌△

VIII. DRILLING ON THE
MOST COMMON SYLLABLES

△ In Chinese, as in other languages, some syllables occur more often than others. The following are the 14 syllables most commonly used in the Chinese language. They are used so often that not a single sentence is spoken without at least one of them.

The 14 syllables are:

1. **de**	wǒ**de** shū	我的书
	xiě**de** xìn	写的信
	pǎo**de** kuài	跑得快
	zhǎng**de** gāo	长得高

2. shi	bàngōngshì	办公室
	tā shì shéi	他是谁
	èrshí suì	二十岁
	shì-yi-shì	试一试
3. yi	dì-yī míng	第一名
	yíge rén	一个人
	yǐwéi	以为
	yīfu	衣服
4. bu	bùxíng	不行
	chàbuduō	差不多
	bùxié	布鞋
	wàijiāobù	外交部
5. you	yǒu shénme shì?	有什么事
	yǒu rén zhǎo nǐ	有人找你
	yòu hǎo yòu kuài	又好又快
	méiyǒu qìyóu	没有汽油
6. zhi	zhīshi	知识
	zhǐyǒu	只有
	sānzhī bǐ	三支笔
	yìzhí zǒu	一直走
7. le	tīng dǒngle	听懂了
	huā hóngle	花红了
	chīle fàn	吃了饭
	jiù zǒule	就走了
8. ji	tā jǐ suì	他几岁
	jǐ hào lóu	几号楼
	jì fēng xìn	寄封信
	zuò fēijī	坐飞机

9. zhe	názhe shū	拿着书
	xiàozhe shuō	笑着说
	zhèjian shì	这件事
	zhèxie rén	这些人
10. wo	wǒ chī	我吃
	wǒ kàn	我看
	wǒmen	我们
	wò shǒu	握手
11. ren	rénkǒu	人口
	kèren	客人
	rènshi	认识
	rènzhēn	认真
12. li	lí jiā jìn	离家近
	zài lǐmian	在里面
	líkai tā	离开他
	qù lǐfà	去理发
13. ta	tā bú qù	他不去
	gàosu tā	告诉他
	tāmen lái	他们来
	xǐhuan tā	喜欢他
14. dao	xiǎo dāo	小刀
	dǎole	倒了
	dédào	得到
	dàole	到了

The following are 33 more syllables commonly used.

15. zhong	zhōngjiān	中间
	duō zhòng	多重
	zhǒngzhǒng	种种

14

16. zi	hànzì	汉字
	fángzi	房子
	zìjǐ	自己
17. guo	guójiā	国家
	shuǐguǒ	水果
	guòqù	过去
18. shang	shāngdiàn	商店
	lóushàng	楼上
	shàngkè	上课
19. ge	liǎngge	两个
	dàgē	大哥
	gèguó	各国
20. men	ménkǒu	门口
	rénmen	人们
	zánmen	咱们
21. he	tā hé nǐ	他和你
	hē shuǐ	喝水
	héshì	合适
22. wei	wèi shénme	为什么
	wèile	为了
	wèishēng	卫生
23. ye	yèli	夜里
	yě qù	也去
	shùyè	树叶
24. da	dàxuéshēng	大学生
	dǎ diànhuà	打电话
	qǐng huídá	请回答

25. gong	gōngyè	工业
	gōngfu	工夫
	yígòng	一共
26. jiu	jiǔ nián	九年
	jiù lái	就来
	hē jiǔ	喝酒
27. jian	kànjian	看见
	shíjiān	时间
	jiànkāng	健康
28. xiang	xiāngzi	箱子
	xiǎngdao	想到
	xiàngqián	向前
29. zhu	zhùhè	祝贺
	zhǔrén	主人
	zhù zài nǎr	住在哪儿
30. lai	hòulái	后来
	lái ma	来吗
	láiguo	来过
31. sheng	yīshēng	医生
	shēngbìng	生病
	shènglì	胜利
32. di	dìzhǐ	地址
	dì-sān	第三
	dǐxia	底下
33. zai	xiànzài	现在
	zài zhèr	在这儿
	zàisān	再三

34.	ni	nǐde	你的
		nǐmen	你们
		nǐ hǎo	你好
35.	xiao	xiāoxi	消息
		hěn xiǎo	很小
		xiàohua	笑话
36.	ke	kěyǐ	可以
		kěnéng	可能
		kěle	渴了
37.	yao	yào shénme	要什么
		yàoshì	要是
		chī yào	吃药
38.	wu	wǔge	五个
		wūzi	屋子
		tiàowǔ	跳舞
39.	yu	xiàyǔ	下雨
		yīngyǔ	英语
		yùdào	遇到
40.	jie	guò jié	过节
		jiē péngyou	接朋友
		jiē diànhuà	接电话
41.	jin	jīntiān	今天
		jìn chéng	进城
		hěn jìn	很近
42.	chan	chǎnshēng	产生
		shēngchǎn	生产
		chǎnpǐn	产品

43. zuo	zuǒbiān	左边
	zuò shénme	做什么
	zuòwèi	座位
44. jia	huàjiā	画家
	jiǎrú	假如
	jiàqī	假期
45. xian	xiānsheng	先生
	xiànmù	羡慕
	xiān zǒu	先走
46. quan	quán bān	全班
	quánshuǐ	泉水
	quànshuō	劝说
47. shuo	shuō Zhōngguóhuà	说中国话
	yào zhème shuō	要这么说
	shuōle yòu shuō	说了又说

The following are 63 syllables commonly used. you will meet them very often though, of course, not so often as the ones listed above.

48. qu	qùnián	去年
	dìqū	地区
49. chu	chūlai	出来
	dàochù	到处
50. er	dì-èr	第二
	érqiě	而且
51. xing	xíngbuxíng	行不行
	xìng shénme	姓什么

52.	hui	huílai	回来
		huìbuhuì	会不会
53.	zheng	zhěngqí	整齐
		zhènghǎo	正好
54.	xi	xībiān	西边
		kàn xì	看戏
55.	dun	yídùn fàn	一顿饭
		liǎngdūn gāng	两吨钢
56.	fu	fùqin	父亲
		zhèngfǔ	政府
57.	jing	jīngcháng	经常
		jǐngchá	警察
58.	na	ná zǒu ba	拿走吧
		nǎr qùle	哪儿去了
59.	fang	fāngbiàn	方便
		fǎngwèn	访问
60.	ba	bāge yuè	八个月
		yǒu bǎwò	有把握
61.	fa	fāxiàn	发现
		fāngfǎ	方法
62.	yuan	yuánlái	原来
		yuànyì	愿意
63.	me	nàme	那么
		zěnmeyàng	怎么样

64.	dong	dǒngxi	东西
		dǒngle	懂了
65.	tong	tóngzhì	同志
		tōngzhī	通知
66.	shu	shūbāo	书包
		shǔ shùr	数数儿
67.	jiao	jiāo xuésheng	教学生
		jiàoshì	教室
68.	mei	méiyǒu	没有
		měige rén	每个人
69.	yang	yángguāng	阳光
		yàngzi	样子
70.	hua	huā kāile	花开了
		shuo huà	说话
71.	yan	yánsè	颜色
		yǎnjing	眼睛
72.	hao	hǎo kàn	好看
		jǐ hào	几号
73.	guan	guān mén	关门
		xíguàn	习惯
74.	hou	shíhou	时候
		yǐhòu	以后
75.	cheng	chénglǐ	城里
		chángchéng	长城

76. xia	xià xīngqī	下星期
	xiàtiān	夏天
77. bian	yìbianr	一边儿
	yíbiàn	一遍
78. ti	tī qiú	踢球
	tǐyù	体育
79. zhao	zhǎo shénme	找什么
	zhàoxiàng	照相
80. dang	dāngrán	当然
	dǎngzhù	挡住
81. wen	wèntí	问题
	wénhuà	文化
82. chang	chàng gē	唱歌
	chángcháng	常常
83. du	shǒudū	首都
	wēndù	温度
84. nian	niánji	年纪
	niàn kèwén	念课文
85. shen	shēntǐ	身体
	hěn shēn	很深
86. ming	míngzì	名字
	míngtiān	明天
87. huo	huódòng	活动
	huǒchē	火车

88. xin	xīnnián	新年
	xìnfēng	信封
89. bi	bíjiào	比较
	bìyè	毕业
90. duo	duōshǎo	多少
	duōme	多么
91. hai	háishì	还是
	dà hǎi	大海
92. dui	duìle	对了
	duìbuqǐ	对不起
93. shou	zuǒ yòu shǒu	左右手
	shòuhuòyuán	售货员
94. xie	xiěxìn	写信
	píxié	皮鞋
95. min	rénmín	人民
	mínzú	民族
96. mian	miànbāo	面包
	jiàn miàn	见面
97. she	shèhuì	社会
	sùshè	宿舍
98. xue	xià xuě	下雪
	xuéyuàn	学院
99. yin	yīnwèi	因为
	yīnyuè	音乐

100. sì	sījī	司机
	sīxiǎng	思想
101. yong	yóuyǒng	游泳
	yòng shénme	用什么
102. qing	qīngchu	清楚
	qǐng zuò	请坐
103. neng	nénggòu	能够
	nénglì	能力
104. qian	yǒu qián	有钱
	qiánbiān	前边
105. tian	tiānqì	天气
	tián biǎo	填表
106. kan	kànjiàn	看见
	zǐxì kàn	仔细看
107. liang	liǎngge rén	两个人
	zhēn liángkuài	真凉快
108. lao	lǎorén	老人
	láodòng	劳动
109. ru	rúguǒ	如果
	rù xué	入学
110. hen	hěn búcùo	很不错
	hǎo de hěn	好得很

Now you are acquainted with the most common syllables in Chinese. They will turn up frequently as you pro-

gress in your Chinese language learning. Be sure to keep each of them in mind.△

You should, first of all, memorize the 14 most common syllables, because you are likely to meet them in any casual remarks you make in Chinese. Suppose you are introducing a friend, you may say, "Tā shì wǒde péngyou." (This is my friend.) This short sentence contains as many as five of the 14 most common Chinese syllables. After listening to the tape, try to make some sentences with these syllables. This will help you memorize them.

Next are the groups of syllables which are less common. Apart from listening to and memorizing them, you are advised to construct a phrase with each sound you hear. Consult the dictionary if you do not trust your memory.

IX. DRILLS ON SYLLABLES ENDING WITH AN ADDED RETROFLEX "ER" SOUND

△Foreign learners of Chinese are often puzzled by an added retroflex "er" sound at the end of some Chinese words.

This is something quite unique to the Chinese language. It is a retroflex "er" sound that follows certain syllables.△

"Er" is sometimes attached to another final to form a retroflex final which is transcribed by adding the letter "-r" to the original final and it is indicated by the character "儿" which follows the preceding one (but it is omitted sometimes), e.g. "wánr" (玩儿), "huàr" (画儿), "xiǎo háir" (小孩儿).

△Here are some of the most common words ending with a retroflex "er" sound.

yīhuìr	一会儿	a little while, in a moment
duōhuìr	多会儿	when; ever; at any time
zhèhuìr	这会儿	now; at the moment; at present
nàhuìr	那会儿	at that time; then
yìbànr	一半儿	one half, in part
duōbànr	多半儿	the greater part; most likely; probably
yìdiǎnr	一点儿	a bit; a little
yǒudiǎnr	有点儿	some; a little; somewhat
nánháir	男孩儿	boy
nǚháir	女孩儿	girl
xiǎoháir	小孩儿	child
wánr	玩儿	play; have fun; amuse oneself

The retroflex "er" sound of some of these words may even have the function of showing a different meaning from the same word without this ending. For example:

diǎn cài 点菜 (to **order** the dishes)	diǎn yíge **diǎnr** 点一个点儿 (to make a **dot**)
quān dì 圈地 (to **enclose** land)	quān yíge **quānr** 圈一个圈儿 (to draw a **circle**)
gài fáng 盖房 (to **build** a house)	gài shang **gàir** 盖上盖儿 (to cover with a **lid**)
huà tú 画图 (to **draw** a chart)	huà yìzhāng **huàr** 画一张画儿 (to draw a **picture**)
huā qián 花钱 (to **spend** money)	zhòng yì péng **huār** 种一盆花儿 (to plant **flowers** in the pot)

25

tān-kāi (to **spread**)	摊开	bǎi ge **tānr** (to keep a **stall**)	摆个摊儿
zuò xià (to **sit** down)	坐下	zhǎo ge **zuòr** (to find a **seat**)	找个坐儿
zháo **huǒ** (to catch **fire**)	着火	tā **huǒr**le (to get **angry**)	他火儿了
huóle (to come back to **life**)	活了	gàn **huór** (to do **work**)	干活儿
yì**bǎ** (a **handful** of)	一把	mén**bàr** (a door-knob)	门把儿
kòng dì (**vacant** ground)	空地	nǐ yǒu **kòngr** ma? (Do you have **time**?)	你有空儿吗？
yí **kuài** (a **piece** of . . .)	一块	yí**kuàir** (**together**)△	一块儿

"-R" is not a syllabic sound. Its basic function is to end the syllable which precedes it with a retroflex, thus changing the quality of the final vowel or the final consonant. For example, "孩" is pronounced "hái", but "小孩儿" should be pronounced "xiǎohár", omitting the final "-i" in the vowel sound. Another example, "盘" is pronounced "pán", but "盘儿" is pronounced "pár", omitting the final consonant "-n". In order to understand spoken Chinese fully, learners are advised to take notice of these sound changes.

X. MODEL DISYLLABIC TONE COMBINATIONS

△Now that you have learned something about rhythm in Chinese, you have probably noticed that it occurs with groups of sounds consisting of two syllables. There are 20 groups of disyllabic tone combinations in the Chinese language. For your convenience, we have worked out a list of Model Disyllabic Tone Combinations. Now listen to this:

Tone 1+1	Tone 1+2	Tone 1+3	Tone 1+4	Tone 1+0
tā tīng	tā lái	tā zǒu	tā qù	tāde
他听	他来	他走	他去	他的

Tone 2+1	Tone 2+2	Tone 2+3	Tone 2+4	Tone 2+0
shéi tīng	shéi lái	shéi zǒu	shéi qù	shéide
谁听	谁来	谁走	谁去	谁的

Tone 3+1	Tone 3+2	Tone 3+3	Tone 3+4	Tone 3+0
wǒ tīng	wǒ lái	wǒ zǒu	wǒ qù	wǒde
我听	我来	我走	我去	我的

Tone 4+1	Tone 4+2	Tone 4+3	Tone 4+4	Tone 4+0
kuài tīng	kuài lái	kuài zǒu	kuài qù	kuàide
快听	快来	快走	快去	快的

The foreign learner of Chinese is often troubled by not being able to use the right tone. It's a bit like singing out of tune. If you have trouble, we advise you to listen to this list of tone combinations once more:

Tone 1+1	Tone 2+1	Tone 3+1	Tone 4+1
tā tīng	shéi tīng	wǒ tīng	kuài tīng
他听	谁听	我听	快听

Tone 1+2	Tone 2+2	Tone 3+2	Tone 4+2
tā lái	shéi lái	wǒ lái	kuài lái
他来	谁来	我来	快来

Tone 1+3	Tone 2+3	Tone 3+3	Tone 4+3
tā zǒu	shéi zǒu	wǒ zǒu	kuài zǒu
他走	谁走	我走	快走
Tone 1+4	**Tone 2+4**	**Tone 3+4**	**Tone 4+4**
tā qù	shéi qù	wǒ qù	kuài qù
他去	谁去	我去	快去
Tone 1+0	**Tone 2+0**	**Tone 3+0**	**Tone 4+0**
tāde	shéide	wǒde	kuàide
他的	谁的	我的	快的△

In spoken Chinese, the difference in tone makes a difference in meaning. A wrong tone is, therefore, misleading. For example, in these two sentences, "Wǒ yào mǎi mǐ." (I want to buy some rice.) and "Wǒ yào mǎi mì." (I want to buy some honey.) although "mǐ" (rice) and "mì" (honey) are the same in initial and final, they are different in tone. While shopping, you might be shown something other than what you intend to buy, just because you did not get the tone of the word right. So, getting the right tone is of primary importance to the learner of Chinese.

The syllables listed here set the standard for tones. You are advised to read them aloud at least twice a day until you know them as well as you know the eight notes on the music scale.

XI. DRILLING ON THE DISYLLABIC TONE COMBINATIONS

Disyllabic rhythm is one of the important features in the Chinese language. There are altogether 20 such disyllabic tone combinations. Now we give four examples for each of them. They are words and phrases in common daily use. Listen to them first, then find their meanings in your glossary. When you have learned their meanings, listen to the tape once again and check whether you can tell the meaning of each on hearing it. If you get one-third of them wrong, you will have to listen to the tape all over again.

△Let's go over the 20 disyllabic tone combinations together:

1st tone + another 1st tone

cānguān	qīngchūn	Fēizhōu	gōngsī
参观	青春	非洲	公司

1st tone + 2nd tone

gōngyuán	ānquán	jiātíng	gāngcái
公园	安全	家庭	刚才

1st tone + 3rd tone

wēnnuǎn	gāngbǐ	kāishǐ	fāngfǎ
温暖	钢笔	开始	方法

1st tone + 4th tone

shēngrì	jīdàn	ānjìng	bāngzhù
生日	鸡蛋	安静	帮助

1st tone + a neutral tone

dāozi	gūniang	chuānghu	shūfu
刀子	姑娘	窗户	舒服

2nd tone + 1st tone

guójiā	dú shū	chénggōng	huáng huā
国家	读书	成功	黄花

2nd tone + another 2nd tone

xuéxí	shítáng	yóujú	huídá
学习	食堂	邮局	回答

2nd tone + 3rd tone

píngguǒ	chuántǒng	érqiě	píjiǔ
苹果	传统	而且	啤酒

2nd tone + 4th tone

jiémù	qúnzhòng	shíyuè	yuánliàng
节目	群众	十月	原谅

2nd tone + a neutral tone

chúle	piányi	háizi	péngyou
除了	便宜	孩子	朋友

3rd tone + 1st tone

jiǎndān	lǎoshī	xiǎoshuō	Běijīng
简单	老师	小说	北京

3rd tone + 2nd tone

ǒurán	Měiguó	yǔyán	yǐqián
偶然	美国	语言	以前

3rd tone + another 3rd tone*

biǎoyǎn	liǎojiě	yǒngyuǎn	xǐzǎo
表演	了解	永远	洗澡

3rd tone + 4th tone

wǎnfàn	yǒuyì	lǐwù	qǐngzuò
晚饭	友谊	礼物	请坐

---

*A 3rd tone when followed by another 3rd tone is pronounced in the 2nd tone, e.g. "nǐ hǎo 你好 —→ ní hǎo".

3rd tone + a neutral tone

zhěntou	diǎnxin	xiǎngxiang	wǎnshang
枕头	点心	想想	晚上

4th tone + 1st tone

dàjiē	chènyī	Aòzhōu	qìchē
大街	衬衣	澳洲	汽车

4th tone + 2nd tone

fùxí	liànxí	dàxué	wàiguó
复习	练习	大学	外国

4th tone + 3rd tone

xiàwǔ	bù shǎo	Rìběn	diànyǐng
下午	不少	日本	电影

4th tone + another 4th tone

dànshì	shuìjiào	àihù	fàndiàn
但是	睡觉	爱护	饭店

4th tone + a neutral tone

cuòle	ànshang	dàifu	kèqi
错了	岸上	大夫	客气

You are probably well acquainted after so much repetition, with the 20 tone combinations. We hope you will find it a lot easier to speak and listen to Chinese now.△

XII. INTENSIVE DRILL ON THE EASILY CONFUSED TONE COMBINATIONS

△You have studied Chinese for quite a while now, but you may still feel a little discouraged at not being able to under-

stand the language properly when other people speak
it. You may want to know why. One of the main reasons
may be that you have confused one tone combination with
another. The following intensive drill on the easily confused
tone combination is designed to help solve this problem.
Please read after us:

(1) **1st tone + 2nd tone**
     dōu lái bāngmáng
     gōngrén dōu lái bāngmáng
     huāyuán gōngrén dōu lái bāngmáng

   1st tone + 3rd tone
     fēngjǐng yōuměi
     cāochǎng fēngjǐng yōuměi
     qīngzǎo cāochǎng fēngjǐng yōuměi

   compare 1st tone + 2nd tone with
   1st tone + 3rd tone
     dōu lái bāngmáng
     fēngjǐng yōuměi
     gōngrén dōu lái bāngmáng
     cāochǎng fēngjǐng yōuměi
     huāyuán gōngrén dōu lái bāngmáng
     qīngzǎo cāochǎng fēngjǐng yōuměi

(2) **2nd tone + another 2nd tone**
     bái-é miányáng
     bái-é miányáng huáng-niú
     bái-é miányáng huáng-niú pá qiáng

2nd tone + 3rd tone
hái yǒu huáng-gǒu
hái yǒu huáng-gǒu hóng-mǎ
hái yǒu huáng-gǒu hóng-mǎ hé wǒ

compare 2nd tone + another 2nd tone with
2nd tone + 3rd tone
bái-é miányáng
hái yǒu huáng-gǒu
bái-é miányáng huáng-níu
hái yǒu huáng-gǒu hóng-mǎ
bái-é miányáng huáng-níu pá qiáng
hái yǒu huáng-gǒu hóng-mǎ hé wǒ

(3) **2nd tone +1st tone**
quán-jiā pá shān
méi fēng quán-jiā pá shān
zuótiān méi fēng quán-jiā pá shān

3rd tone + 1st tone
xiǎng tīng guǎngbō
měitiān xiǎng tīng guǎngbō
lǎoshī měitiān xiǎng tīng guǎngbō

Compare 2nd tone + 1st tone with
3rd tone + 1st tone
quán-jiā pá shān
xiǎng tīng guǎngbō
méi fēng quán-jiā pá shān
měitiān xiǎng tīng guǎngbō
zuótiān méi fēng quán-jiā pá shān
lǎoshī měitiān xiǎng tīng guǎngbō

33

(4) **3rd tone + 2nd tone**
yǒu hóng yǒu bái
xiǎo qiú yǒu hóng yǒu bái
shǒu ná xiǎo qiú yǒu hóng yǒu bái

2nd tone + another 2nd tone
lánqiú páiqiú
cháng wánr lánqiú páiqiú
értóng cháng wánr lánqiú páiqiú

compare 3rd tone + 2nd tone with
2nd tone + another 2nd tone
yǒu hóng yǒu bái
lánqiú páiqiú
xiǎo qiú yǒu hóng yǒu bái
cháng wánr lánqiú páiqiú
shǒu ná xiǎo qiú yǒu hóng yǒu bái
értóng cháng wánr lánqiú páiqiú

(5) **3rd tone + 4th tone**
wǒ qù pǎobù
bǐsài wǒ qù pǎobù
jiǔyuè bǐsài wǒ qù pǎobù

2nd tone + 4th tone
yúkuài jiéshù
huódòng yúkuài jiéshù
guóqìng huódòng yúkuài jiéshù

compare 3rd tone + 4th tone with
2nd tone + 4th tone
wǒ qù pǎobù

yúkuài jiéshù
bǐsài wǒ qù pǎobù
huódòng yúkuài jiéshù
jiǔyuè bǐsài wǒ qù pǎobù
guóqìng huódòng yúkuài jiéshù

(6)   4th tone + 2nd tone
tèbié rèqíng
shàonián tèbié rèqíng
fàngniú shàonián tèbié rèqíng

4th tone + 3rd tone
zuì hǎo yòng nǎo
yòng yǎn zuì hǎo yòng nǎo
yòng shǒu yòng yǎn zuì hǎo yòng nǎo

compare 4th tone + 2nd tone with
4th tone + 3rd tone
tèbié rèqíng
zuì hǎo yòng nǎo
shàonián tèbié rèqíng
yòng yǎn zuì hǎo yòng nǎo
fàngniú shàonián tèbié rèqíng
yòng shǒu yòng yǎn zuì hǎo yòng nǎo

(7)   4th tone + 3rd tone
jìzhě dàibiǎo
sòng-zǒu jìzhě dàibiǎo
xiàozhǎng sòng-zǒu jìzhě dàibiǎo

2nd tone + 3rd tone
méiyǒu xué-hǎo

cóngxiǎo méiyǒu xué-hǎo
déyǔ cóngxiǎo méiyǒu xué-hǎo

**compare 4th tone + 3rd tone with
2nd tone + 3rd tone**

jìzhě dàibiǎo
méiyǒu xué-hǎo
sòng-zǒu jìzhě dàibiǎo
cóngxiǎo méiyǒu xué hǎo
xiàozhǎng sòng-zǒu jìzhě dàibiǎo
déyǔ cóngxiǎo méiyǒu xué-hǎo

(8) **4th tone + another 4th tone**
kèwài zuòyè
zài zuò kèwài zuòyè
xiàkè zài zuò kèwài zuòyè

1st tone + 4th tone
jīnrì dōu zuò
gōngzuò jīnrì dōu zuò
jīnrì gōngzuò jīnrì dōu zuò

**compare 4th tone + another 4th tone with
1st tone + 4th tone**
kèwài zuòyè
jīnrì dōu zuò
zài zuò kèwài zuòyè
gōngzuò jīnrì dōu zuò
xiàkè zài zuò kèwài zuòyè
jīnrì gōngzuò jīnrì dōu zuò

(9) **compare 1st tone + a neutral tone with**
     4th tone + a neutral tone

duōme	zhème
bēizi	màozi
dōngxi	àiren
chūqule	xiàqule
tāmen chūqule	àiren xiàqule

(10) **compare 3rd tone + a neutral tone with**
     2nd tone + a neutral tone

zěnme	shénme
yǐzi	érzi
ěrduo	juéde
wǒmen	rénmen
qǐlaile	huílaile
wǒmen qǐlaile	rénmen huílaile△

The results of a listening test on tone discrimination conducted among foreign learners of Chinese show that of the 20 tone combinations 10 are easily confused. Intensive drilling exercise on the 10 easily confused tone combinations are provided here to impress on you their difference. Some of the combinations may prove to be especially difficult for you, but you will achieve a correct reflex after practising them many times without looking at the script.

After an intensive drill like this, you should be able to distinguish the different tones in the tone combinations better. If you are still not too sure, please do the following exercise to test yourself. Place a tone-mark on each syllable representing the different tones as you hear them.

zuguo	songgei	xuanze	yinhang
xinwen	ganmao	queshao	kaishui
chouyan	shoudu	putong	kache
jundui	guanggao	maidao	liwu
xiuxi	niurou	shangwu	qinglang
lüxing	huida	zhongguo	funü
hongde	tamen	feichang	nuanhuo

XIII. A COMPREHENSIVE DRILL ON FINALS, INITIALS AND TONES

△The purpose of this drill is to give you an overall idea of the syllable in Chinese. Please do not look at the tape script while practising. You are required to read with fluency, correct pronunciation and the right use of tones.

Please do this exercise on finals, initials and tones with muse. (An exercise to discriminate the easily confused initials.)

bā-pā	bō-pō	gē-kē	gāi-kāi
nú-lú	niú-liú	jú-qú	jué-qué
zhěn-chěn	zhěng-chěng	suǐ-shuǐ	sǒu-shǒu
dào-tào	dòu-tòu	zuò-cuò	zài-cài

gǎnkuài 赶快	gōngkè 功课	cūnzi 村子	zǎocāo 早操
chēzhàn 车站	zhèngcháng 正常	dàitì 代替	táidēng 台灯
jīqì 机器	qiánjìn 前进	zázhì 杂志	chǐcùn 尺寸
juéxīn 决心	quánxīn 全新	zháojí 着急	chūqu 出去
pángbiān 旁边	pǎobù 跑步		

cāi yi cāi, zǒu yi zǒu,

bào yi bào, pǎo yi pǎo,

zhǎngde cháng, kāide hǎo.

compare and practise

(An exercise to discriminate the easily confused finals.)

ān-āng	ēn-ēng	in-ing	ēng-ōng
bēn-bēng	néng-nóng	lǎn-lǎng	qìn-qìng
xiāo-xiū	yáo-yóu	huǒ-hǒu	wài-wèi
mó-móu	qián-quán	xiǎn-xiǎng	qún-qióng
shān-shuān-shuāng		fán-fén-féng	

jiānqiáng 坚强　jìnxíng 进行　guānguāng观光

kuānguǎng宽广　yǎnyuán演员　zhēnzhèng真正　yǔyī 雨衣

qiányán 前言　yǒuhǎo 友好　chāoguò 超过　zhēnzhǔn真准

tóngděng 同等

compare and practise

(A drill on the combination of initials, finals and tones.)

zhēn gāo真高	zhēn cháng 真长	zhēn yuǎn真远	zhēn jìn真近
hái gāo 还高	hái cháng 还长	hái yuǎn 还远	hái jìn 还近
hěn gāo 很高	hěn cháng 很长	hěn yuǎn 很远	hěn jìn 很近
tài gāo 太高	tài cháng 太长	tài yuǎn 太远	tài jìn 太近
bù gāo 不高	bù cháng 不长	bù yuǎn 不远	bú jìn 不近

　　jiāng-shān duō-jiāo

　　níu-yáng chéng-qún

　　měihǎo yuǎnjing

　　bìanhuàn mò-cè

　　huā-hóng liǔ-lù

shān-míng shuǐ-xiù
shēn-qiáng tǐ-zhuàng
xīn-míng yǎn-liàng
dà-hǎo héshān
wàn-gǔ liú-fāng
rè-huǒ cháo-tiān
yào-wǔ yáng-wēi
tāde gēge cā zhuōzi
bóbo pópo bá luóbo
wǒde nǎinai mǎi guǒzi
dìdi mèimei gài bèizi△

XIV. TESTING

△We are coming to the end of this cassette tape. By now you should have gained much more confidence in learning the Chinese language than you had at the beginning of this course, and we hope that you have been enjoying it. If you can finish the following check-up exercises without much difficulty, you will see for yourself how much you have achieved in this short space of time. Congratulations and good luck to you!

Dictation

Write down the initial and final combinations according to the sounds you hear

zhīdào—chídào   běnzi—pénzi

dìtú—túdi   zàijiàn—cái jiàn

kāifàn—kāifàng   yùn shuǐ—yòng shuǐ

jīnyú—jīngyú   guāfēn—guā fēng

bú xìn—bú xìng   xūnzhāng—xiōngzhāng

shān xià—sān xiàr   gōngchǎng—kòng chǎng

mùchuán—mùchuáng   xiānhuā—xiānghuā

lúnzi—lóngzi

Connect the initials and the finals, according to what you have heard.

b	ei	q	iong
p	en	z	i
d	ing	c	ü
n	eng	s	u
g	an	zh	ao
k	in	sh	e
l	ui	x	ou
r	ong	y	ün
j	uo		

Fill in each of the blanks with the correct initials.

(z) (c)

__āochǎng shang rén hěn duō.

(b) (p)

Xiànzài shì __ā diǎn __ àn.

(zh) (ch)

Nǐ qù __ī fàn ma?

(d) (t)

41

Zhè liǎng __ iān méiyǒu __ àiyang.

  (g) (k)

Tā __ ùnle.

  (j) (q)

Zhè shì __ īshí __ iǔ.

Listen to the following sentence twice and tell how many neutral tones there are in it.

    Tiān-shangde rìtou, dì-xiade shítou, zuǐ-lide shétou.

Listen to the following tongue-twister several times and try to repeat it by yourself.

    Sì shì sì, shí shì shí, shísì shì shísì, sìshí shì sìshí.

    Hóng fènghuang, fěn fènghuang, fěn-hóng fènghuang.

After practising the two tongue-twisters, make a recording of your performance and then compare it with the tape. △

KEY TO THE EXERCISES

(See p. 38)

zǔguó	sònggěi	xuǎnzé	yínháng
xīnwén	gǎnmào	quēshǎo	kāishuǐ
chōuyān	shǒudū	pǔtōng	kǎchē
jūnduì	guǎnggào	mǎidào	lǐwù
xiūxi	niúròu	shàngwǔ	qínglǎng
lǚxíng	huídá	zhōngguó	fùnǚ
hóngde	tāmen	fēicháng	nuǎnhuo

*　　*　　*

(See pp. 40-42)

Dictation

zuòcāo	ménfèng	zhànchǎng	qīngxìn
niánlíng	sùshè	liǎo bu qǐ	bízi
bàopò	yuèliang	tīng dǒng	gāokǎo

Write down the initial and final combinations according to the sounds you hear.

zhīdào	běnzi	dìtú	zàijiàn
kāifàn	yòng shuǐ	jīnyú	guā fēng
bú xìn	xiōngzhāng	shān xià	kòng chǎng
mùchuáng	xiānghuā	lóngzi	

Connect the initials and the finals according to what you have heard.

beng	qu
pen	zu
dan	ce
nin	sao
gei	zhuo
kong	shou
ling	xiong
rui	yun
ji	

Fill in each of the blanks with the correct initials.

Cāochǎng shang rén hěn duō.

Xiànzài shì bā diǎn bàn.

Nǐ qù chī fàn ma?

Zhè liǎng tiān méiyǒu tàiyang.

Tā kùnle.

Zhè shì qīshí jiǔ.

Listen to the following sentence twice and tell how many neutral tones there are in it.

9. —shang, de, tou, xia, de, tou, li, de, tou.

GLOSSARY

A

ai

ài	爱	love, like
àihù	爱护	cherish, treasure
àiren	爱人	husband or wife, sweetheart

an

ānjìng	安静	quiet, peaceful
ānquán	安全	safe
ànshang	岸上	on the bank

ang

āngzāng	肮脏	dirty, filthy

ao

Aòzhōu	澳洲	Australia

B

ba

bā	八	eight
bā diǎn bàn	八点半	half past eight (o'clock)
bāge yuè	八个月	eight months
bāyuè	八月	August
bá	拔	pull out, pull up
bá luóbo	拔萝卜	pull out a radish
bàba	爸爸	papa, dad

bai

bái	白	white
báicài	白菜	Chinese cabbage

45

bái-é	白鹅	white goose
bǎi	摆	put, place, arrange
bǎi ge tānr	摆个摊儿	set up a stall
ban		
bàn	办	manage, handle
bàngōngshì	办公室	office
bang		
bāngmáng	帮忙	help
bāngzhù	帮助	help, assist
bao		
bào	报	newspaper, report
bàodǎo	报导	report (news)
bàopò	爆破	blow up, demolish, dynamite, blast
bào yi bào	抱一抱	hold in the arms
bei		
bēizi	杯子	cup, glass
běi	北	north
Běi-Měi	北美	North America
ben		
běnzi	本子	notebook
bi		
bízi	鼻子	nose
bǐjiào	比较	compare, contrast, comparatively
bǐsài	比赛	match, competition, contest

46

bìyè	毕业	graduate, finish school
bian		
biàn	变	change, become different
biànhuàn mò-cè	变幻莫测	changeable, unpredictable
biao		
biǎo	表	table (as multiplication table), wrist watch
biǎoyǎn	表演	perform, play, act, performing
bie		
biéde	别的	other
bo		
bóbo	伯伯	father's elder brother, uncle
bōli	玻璃	glass
bómó	薄膜	membrane, film
bu		
bù*	不	no, not
bùcháng	不长	not long
búcuò	不错	not bad, pretty good
bùgāo	不高	not high
bújìn	不近	not near
búqù	不去	not going
bùshǎo	不少	not few

---

*"不" is pronounced in the 4th tone (bù) when it stands by itself or precedes a 1st, 2nd or 3rd tone, but is pronounced in the 2nd tone (bú) when it precedes a 4th tone.

búxìn	不信	not believe, no confi-dence
búxìng	不幸	unfortunate
bùxíng	不行	won't do, be no good, not work
bùyuǎn	不远	not far

C

ca
| cā | 擦 | rub, wipe, brush, shave |
| cā zhuōzi | 擦桌子 | wipe the table |

cai
| cái | 才 | then and only then |
| cāi yi cāi | 猜一猜 | guess |

can
| cānguān | 参观 | visit (a place) |
| cānjiā | 参加 | join, take part in |

cao
| cāochǎng | 操场 | playground, sportsfield |
| cǎo | 草 | grass, straw |

cha
| chà buduō | 差不多 | almost, almost the same |

chan
| chǎnpǐn | 产品 | product |
| chǎnshēng | 产生 | produce, bring forth, generate |

chang
| chángcháng | 常常 | often, usually |

cháng	长	long
cháng chéng	长城	the Great Wall
chàng gē	唱歌	sing
cháng wánr	常玩儿	often play
chao		
cháo	朝	towards, facing
chāoguò	超过	surpass, exceed
che		
chē	车	vehicle
chēzhàn	车站	station, depot, stop
chen		
chènyī	衬衣	underclothes, shirt
cheng		
chéng chē	乘车	take a bus
chénggōng	成功	succeed
chénglǐ	城里	inside the city, in town
chi		
chī	吃	eat
chī fàn	吃饭	have a meal
chī yào	吃药	take medicine
chídào	迟到	come (or arrive) late
chǐ	尺	ruler
chǐcùn	尺寸	measurement, dimensions, size
chu		
chūlai	出来	come out, emerge
chūqu	出去	go out, get out
chúle	除了	except, besides

49

chuan

chuántǒng	传统	tradition

chuang

chuāng	窗	window
chuānghu	窗户	window, casement
chuāngkuàng	窗框	window frame

cong

cóng	从	from, through
cóngcǐ	从此	from now on, from then on
cōngming	聪明	intelligent, clever
cōngxiǎo	从小	from childhood, as a child

cui

cuīhuǐ	摧毁	destroy, smash, wreck

cun

cūnzi	村子	village

cuo

cuòle	错了	wrong, mistaken, erroneous

D

da

dā	搭	put up
dá	答	answer
dǎ	打	strike, beat
dǎ diànhuà	打电话	make a phone call
dà	大	big, large
dàgē	大哥	elder brother
dàhǎi	大海	sea

50

dàjiē	大街	street, main street
dàmā	大妈	aunt, father's elder brother's wife
dàxué	大学	university
dàxuésheng	大学生	student
dai		
dàibiǎo	代表	represent, representative
dàifu	大夫	doctor
dàitì	代替	replace, substitute for
dan		
dànshì	但是	but
dang		
dāngrán	当然	of course, naturally
dǎngzhù	挡住	keep off, ward off
dao		
dāozi	刀子	knife
dàochù	到处	everywhere
dǎole	倒了	have fallen
dàole	到了	have arrived, arrived
de		
de*	的	*a structural particle*

---

*(1) When a noun or a pronoun is used as an attributive to show possession, the structural particle "的" must be inserted between the attributive and what it qualifies. (2) A verb, verbal construction or subject-predicate construction, when used as an attributive, must take after it the structural particle "的". (3) With the structural particle "的", an adjective can be used as the modifier of a noun or to stand for the noun it modifies with the noun omitted.

51

dédào	得到	get, obtain, gain, receive
déyǔ	德语	German (language)
děngdeng	等等	and so on and so forth, etc.

di

dìdi	弟弟	younger brother
dì-èr	第二	second
dìqū	地区	prefecture, district, area
dì-sān	第三	third
dìtú	地图	map
dǐxià	底下	underneath, under
dìxià	地下	on the ground, (under-ground)
dì-yīmíng	第一名	first place, number one
dìzhǐ	地址	address

dian

diǎn	点	drop, dot, spot
diǎn cài	点菜	choose dishes from a menu, order dishes (in a restaurant)
diǎn yīge diǎnr	点一个点儿	put a dot
diǎnxin	点心	light refreshments, pastry
diàn	电	electricity
diànxiàn	电线	(electric) wire
diànyǐng	电影	film, movie

dong

dōng	东	east
dōngxi	东西	thing

dǒngle	懂了	understand, know
dou		
dōu	都	all
dōu lái	都来	all come
du		
dú	读	read, study
dú shū	读书	read the book
duan		
duǎn	短	short, brief
duànliàn	锻练	take exercise, have physical training, temper, steel
dui		
duìbuqǐ	对不起	sorry
duìle	对了	all right, correct
duo		
duō	多	many, much, more
duōbànr	多半儿	the greater part, most
duōhuìr	多会儿	whenever, at any time
duōme	多么	how
duōshǎo	多少	how many, how much
duōzhòng	多重	how heavy, how much does . . . weigh

E

er		
érqiě	而且	moreover, besides, and
értóng	儿童	children

érzi	儿子	son
ěrduo	耳朵	ear
èr*	二	two
èrshí suì	二十岁	twenty years old

F

fa

| fāxiàn | 发现 | find, discover |

fan

| fàn | 饭 | meal, cooked rice |
| fàndiàn | 饭店 | hotel, restaurant |

fang

fāng	方	square
fāngfǎ	方法	method
fāngxiàng	方向	direction
fángzi	房子	house
fǎngwèn	访问	visit, call on, interview
fàng niú	放牛	pasture (or graze) cattle

fei

fēi	飞	fly, flit
fēijī	飞机	aircraft, plane
fēicháng	非常	extremely, unusual
Fēizhōu	非洲	Africa

---

*Both "二" (èr) and "两" (liǎng) mean two, but they are not interchangeable: (1) "二" is used as the ordinal number, e.g. 二月 (èr yuè), 第二课 (dì-èr kè). (2) As the last digit of a number larger than ten, "二" is used, e.g. 十二 (shí-èr), 三十二 (sānshí-èr), 二百零二 (èrbǎi líng èr). . . .

fen

fēn	分	divide, part, separate
fěn	粉	powder
fěnhóng	粉红	pink

feng

fēng	风	wind
fēngfù	丰富	rich, abundant, plentiful
fènghuáng	凤凰	phoenix
fēngjing	风景	scenery, landscape
fēngzheng	风筝	kite

fu

fùnǚ	妇女	woman
fúwù	服务	serve
fùqin	父亲	father
fùxí	复习	review, revise

G

gai

gài	盖	lid, cover
gài bèizi	盖被子	cover . . . with a quilt
gài fángzi	盖房子	build a house
gàishang gàir	盖上盖儿	cover . . . with the lid

gan

gǎn	赶	catch up with
gǎnkuài	赶快	hurriedly, be quick
gǎnmào	感冒	catch cold, have a cold
gǎntàn	感叹	sigh with feeling
gàn	干	do, work
gàn huór	干活儿	work on a job, labour

gang

gāng	钢	steel
gāngbǐ	钢笔	pen, fountain pen
gāngcái	刚才	just now, a moment ago

gao

gāo	高	high, tall
gāokǎo	高考	entrance examination for institutions of higher learning
gāoxìng	高兴	glad, happy, pleased
gàosu	告诉	tell, let know

ge

gē	歌	song
gēbo	胳膊	arm
gēge	哥哥	elder brother
gè*	个	*a measure word*
gè	各	each, every
gèguó	各国	each country

gen

gēn	根	root
gēnběn	根本	basic, fundamental

gong

gōngchǎng	工厂	factory
gōngfu	工夫	workmanship, time
gōngkè	功课	homework, schoolwork
gōngnóng	工农	workers and peasants

---

*In modern Chinese, every noun, as a rule, has its specific measure word. "个" is the most extensively used of all and can apply to a person as well as a thing.

gōngrén	工人	worker
gōngsī	公司	company, corporation
gōngyuán	公园	park
gōngyè	工业	industry
gōngzuò	工作	work, job
gu		
gūniang	姑娘	girl, daughter
gua		
guā	瓜	melon, gourd
guāfēn	瓜分	carve up, divide up
guā fēng	刮风	blow wind
guan		
guān	关	shut, close
guānguāng	观光	go sightseeing, visit
guān mén	关门	shut the door
guang		
guāng	光	light, ray
guǎng	广	broad, wide, vast, extensive
guǎngbō	广播	broadcast
guǎnggào	广告	advertisement
guo		
guó	国	country, state, nation
guójiā	国家	country
guóqìng	国庆	national day
guò	过	cross, past
guòqū	过去	(in or of) the past, former, previously
guǒzi	果子	fruit

H

hai

hái	还	still, yet, even, also
hái cháng	还长	longer, still too long
hái gāo	还高	higher, still too high
hái jìn	还近	closer, still too close
hái yuǎn	还远	farther, still too far
háishì	还是	still, after all, or (used in questions)
háiyǒu	还有	besides . . . there is (are)
háizi	孩子	child

han

Hànyǔ	汉语	Chinese (language)
Hànzì	汉字	Chinese character

hao

hǎo	好	good, well
hǎo de hěn	好得很	very good
hǎokàn	好看	good-looking, nice

he

hē	喝	drink
hē jiǔ	喝酒	drink wine
hē shuǐ	喝水	drink water
hé*	和	and, with
hégé	合格	qualified, up to standard

---

*The conjunction "和" is not the same as English "and". "和" can only be used between words or phrases, but not clauses.

héshì	合适	suitable, appropriate
héshuǐ	河水	river
hen		
hěn	很	very, quite
hěn búcuò	很不错	not bad, pretty good
hěn cháng	很长	very long
hěn duō	很多	very much
hěn gāo	很高	very high
hěn hǎo	很好	very good
hěn jìn	很近	very near
hěn shēn	很深	very deep
hěn xiǎo	很小	very small, very little
hěn yuǎn	很远	very far
hong		
hóngde	红的	red
hóng mǎ	红马	red horse
hou		
hòu	后	behind, back, after
hòulái	后来	afterwards, later
hua		
huār	花儿	flower, blossom, bloom
huāduǒ	花朵	flower
huā-hong liǔ-lǜ	花红柳绿	red flowers and green willows, beautiful scenery
huā kāile	花开了	the flowers are blooming
huā hóngle	花红了	the flowers are red
huà	画	draw, paint

59

huàr	画儿	drawing, picture
huà yìzhāng huàr	画一张画儿	draw a picture
huà yìduǒ huār	画一朵花儿	draw a flower
huang		
huáng	黄	yellow
huáng gǒu	黄狗	brown dog
huáng huār	黄花	yellow flower
huáng níu	黄牛	yellow ox, cattle
hui		
huídá	回答	answer, reply
huílái	回来	return, come back
huílaile	回来了	have come back
huì bu huì	会不会	are you able to ..., can you ...
huo		
huó	活	live, alive
huór	活儿	work
huódòng	活动	move about, activity
huóle	活了	alive, living
huǒ	火	fire
huǒchē	火车	train
huǒr	火儿	anger, temper, flare up

J

ji		
jī	鸡	chicken
jīdàn	鸡蛋	(hen's) egg
jīqì	机器	machine

jǐ*	几	how many, several
jǐge	几个	how many, several
jǐhào	几号	which number
jǐhào lóu	几号楼	which building
jì	寄	send, post, mail
jì fēng xìn	寄封信	post a letter
jì	记	remember, bear in mind, record, notes, mark
jìzhě	记者	newsman, reporter
jia		
jiā	家	home, family
jiātíng	家庭	family, household
jiǎ	假	false
jiǎrú	假如	if, suppose that
jiǎyá	假牙	denture, false tooth
jiàqī	假期	vacation, holidays
jian		
jiǎndān	简单	simple
jiànkāng	健康	healthy
jiàn miàn	见面	meet, see
jiānqiáng	坚强	undaunted, strong
jiang		
jiāng	江	river
jiāngshān	江山	landscape, rivers and mountains

---

*When asking any number under 10, the interrogative pronoun "几" (jǐ) is usually used. A measure word is necessary between "几" and the noun it qualifies since "几" stands for a numeral.

jiāngshān duō-jiāo 江山多娇		beautiful landscape
jiao		
jiāo	教	teach, instruct
jiāo xuésheng	教学生	to teach students
jiàoshì	教室	classroom
jie		
jiē	接	connect, contact
jiē diànhuà	接电话	to answer the phone
jiē péngyou	接朋友	to receive a friend
jiějie	姐姐	elder sister
jiémù	节目	programme, item
jiéshù	结束	finish, end, conclude
jin		
jīnrì	今日	today
jīntiān	今天	today
jīnyú	金鱼	gold fish
jìn	进	advance, enter
jìn chéng	进城	go to town
jìn xíng	进行	carry out, be in progress
jing		
jīngcháng	经常	frequently, constantly
jīngyú	鲸鱼	whale
jǐngchá	警察	policeman
jiu		
jiǔ	九	nine
jiǔliú	久留	stay for a long time
jiǔ nián	九年	nine years
jiǔyuè	九月	September

jiùjiu	舅舅	mother's brother
jiù	就	then, and so
jue		
juéde	觉得	feel
juéxīn	决心	determined, determination
jun		
jūnduì	军队	army, troop
jūnyǔn	均匀	even, well-distributed

K

kai		
kāi	开	open
kāi chē	开车	drive (a car, train, etc.)
kāide hǎo	开得好	be good at driving
kāi fàn	开饭	serve a meal
kāifàng	开放	be open
kāishǐ	开始	begin, start
kāishuǐ	开水	boiled water
kan		
kàn	看	look, watch, see
kànjiàn	看见	see, catch sight of
kàn xì	看戏	go to the theatre, see a play (an opera, etc.)
ke		
kěkào	可靠	reliable
kěle	渴了	be thirsty
kěnéng	可能	possible, maybe

kèqi	客气	polite
kèren	客人	guest, visitor
kèwài	课外	outside class, after school
kěyǐ	可以	can, may, pretty good

kong

kōng	空	empty, hollow
kòngchǎng	空场	empty space
kòngdì	空地	vacant lot, open ground
kòngr	空儿	empty space, free time, spare time.

kuai

kuàide	快的	fast, quick, rapid
kuài lái	快来	come quickly
kuài qù	快去	go quickly
kuài tīng	快听	be quick to listen
kuài zǒu	快走	walk quickly

kuan

| kuān | 宽 | wide, width |
| kuānguǎng | 宽广 | broad, extensive |

kun

| kùnle | 困了 | be sleepy |
| kūnlún | 昆仑 | the Kunlun Mountains |

L

lai

lái	来	come, arrive
lái guo	来过	have been here (before)
lái le	来了	have come
lái ma	来吗	are you coming

lan

lán	蓝	blue
lánqíu	篮球	basketball

lao

láodòng	劳动	work, labour
lǎo	老	old, aged
lǎolao	姥姥	grandma
lǎorén	老人	the aged, the old
lǎoshī	老师	teacher

le

le*	了	① *a modal particle* ② *an aspect particle*

lei

lèi	累	tired, work hard
lèi ma	累吗	are you tired

li

lí	离	leave, part from
lí jiā jìn	离家近	near one's home
líkāi tā	离开他	to leave him
lǐwù	礼物	gift, present
lǐtáng	礼堂	auditorium

lian

liànxí	练习	practise, exercise

liang

---

*The aspect particle "了" can be added to a verb to show the completion or realization of an action. Put at the end of a sentence, "了" is the most extensively used modal particle which can have several meanings. When it refers to an event that happened some time in the past, it shows that this event did take place.

liǎng*	两	two
liǎng dùn fàn	两顿饭	two meals
liao		
liǎo jiě	了解	understand, find out, know thoroughly
liǎo bu qǐ	了不起	amazing, terrific
liu		
liù	六	six
liùge yuè	六个月	six months
liùyuè	六月	June
long		
lóng	聋	deaf, hard of hearing
lóng zi	聋子	a deaf person
lou		
lóu	楼	storey, floor
lóu shàng	楼上	upstairs
lun		
lúnzi	轮子	wheel
luo		
luōsuo	罗嗦	long-winded, wordy, over elaborate
lü		
lǚxíng	旅行	travel, journey, tour

M

| **ma** | | |
| māma | 妈妈 | mum, mummy |

*Both "二" (èr) and "两" (liǎng) mean 2. When 2 comes before a measure word, "两" (liǎng) is used instead of "二" (èr).

66

mǎ	马	horse
ma*	吗	*an interrogative particle*
mai		
mǎi	买	buy
mǎidào	买到	have bought
mǎi guǒzi	买果子	buy fruits
mài	卖	sell
mao		
mào zi	帽子	hat, cap, headgear
mei		
méi	没	not have
měi	每	every, each, per
méiyǒu	没有	not have, there is not
Měiguó	美国	U.S.A.
měihǎo yuǎnjing	美好远景	magnificent prospects
mèimei	妹妹	younger sister
men		
mén	门	door
ménbàr	门把儿	door-knob
mén fèng	门缝	a crack between a door and its frame
ménkǒu	门口	doorway, entrance
mi		
mǐ	米	rice
mì	蜜	honey
mìmì	秘密	secret, clandestine

---

*When "吗" is added at the end of a declarative sentence, it becomes an interrogative sentence.

mian

miàn	面	face, surface
miànbāo	面包	bread
miányáng	绵羊	sheep

min

mínzhǔ	民主	democracy
mínzú	民族	nation, nationality

ming

míngbai	明白	clear, obvious
míngtian	明天	tomorrow
mìnglìng	命令	order, command
míngzi	名字	name

mu

mùchǎng	牧场	grazing land, pasture
mùchuáng	木床	wooden bed
mùtou	木头	wood

N

na

ná	拿	take (carry) with hand
názhe shū	拿着书	carry a book
ná zǒu	拿走	take away
nǎ	哪	which, what
nǎge	哪个	which
nǎr	哪儿	where
nǎhuìr	哪会儿	when, whenever
nǎr qùle	哪儿去了	where did . . . go
nà	那	that, in that case
nàhuìr	那会儿	at that time

nàme	那么	so, then, in that way
nàr	那儿	there, that place
nai		
nǎi	奶	milk
nǎinai	奶奶	grandma
nan		
nán	男	man, male
nánháir	男孩儿	boy
neng		
néng	能	can, energy
nénggòu	能够	can, be able to
nénglì	能力	ability, capacity
ni		
nǐ	你	you
nǐde	你的	your
nǐ hǎo	你好	how do you do, how are you
nǐmen	你们	you (second person plural)
nǐ qù	你去	you go
nǐ yǒu kòngr ma	你有空儿吗	do you have time
nian		
nián	年	year
niánlíng	年龄	age
niàn	念	read aloud
niàn kèwén	念课文	read the text
niao		
niǎo	鸟	bird

niu

niú	牛	cattle (ox or cow)
niúnǎi	牛奶	cow milk
niú ròu	牛肉	beef

niú-yáng chéng-
   qún
	牛羊成群	a large number of cattle
		   and sheep

nuan

nuǎnhuo	暖和	warm

nü

nǚ	女	woman, female
nǚháir	女孩儿	girl

O

ou

Ouzhōu	欧洲	Europe
ǒurán	偶然	accidental

P

pa

pá	爬	climb, crawl
pá qiáng	爬墙	climb a wall
pá shān	爬山	climb a mountain

pai

páiqíu	排球	volleyball

pang

pángbiān	旁边	side, next to

pao

pǎo	跑	run
pǎo bù	跑步	running

pǎode kuài	跑得快	run fast
pǎo yi pǎo	跑一跑	run
pen		
pén	盆	tub, pot, basin
pénzi	盆子	basin
peng		
péngyou	朋友	friend
pi		
pí	皮	skin, leather
píjiǔ	啤酒	beer
píxié	皮鞋	leather shoes
pian		
piányi	便宜	cheap
pin		
pīnyīn	拼音	spell, phoneticize
ping		
píng	平	flat, level, even, smooth
píngguǒ	苹果	apple
pīngpāng	乒乓	table-tennis
píngjìng	平静	quiet, calm
po		
pópo	婆婆	husband's mother
pu		
pǔbiàn	普遍	universal, widespread
pǔtōng	普通	ordinary, common

Q

| **qi** | | |
| qī | 七 | seven |

qīshí jiǔ	七十九	seventy-nine
qǐlai le	起来了	get up, stand up
qìchē	汽车	automobile, car
qian		
qián	前	front, before, ago
qiánbiān	前边	in front, ahead
qiánjìn	前进	advance, go forward
qiányán	前言	preface, foreword
qin		
qīnqī	亲戚	relative
qing		
qīng	轻	light, not important
qīngxìn	轻信	be credulous
qīngchu	清楚	clear
qīngchūn	青春	youth, young
qīngzǎo	清早	early morning
qínglǎng	晴朗	fine, sunny
qǐng	请	please
qǐng huídá	请回答	answer the question, please
qǐng jìn	请进	come in
qǐng zuò	请坐	sit down, please
qu		
qù	去	go, leave
qù lǐfà	去理发	go and have one's hair cut
qùnián	去年	last year
quan		
quāndì	圈地	to encircle a piece of land

72

quān yīge quǎnr	圈一个圈儿	to draw a circle
quán bān	全班	the whole class
quán jiā	全家	the whole family
quánshuǐ	泉水	spring water
quántǐ	全体	all, entire, whole
quán xīn	全新	brand new
quànshuō	劝说	persuade, advise
que		
quēshǎo	缺少	lack, be short of
qun		
qúnzhòng	群众	masses

R

re

rè	热	heat, hot
rèqíng	热情	enthusiastic, warm
rè-huǒ cháo-tiān	热火朝天	be bustling with activity
ren		
rén	人	person, people
rénkǒu	人口	population
rénmen	人们	people (human beings in general), the public
rénmín	人民	the people
rènshi	认识	know, recognize
rènzhēn	认真	conscientious, earnest
reng		
réngrán	仍然	as usual, as before
ri		
Rìběn	日本	Japan

rìtou	日头	sun
rong		
róngyì	容易	easy
ru		
rúguǒ	如果	if
rù xué	入学	enter school

S

san		
sān	三	three
sān suì	三岁	three years old
sān xiàr	三下儿	three times
sān zhī bǐ	三支笔	three pens (or any other writing instruments)
sang		
sǎngzi	嗓子	throat, voice
shan		
shān	山	hill, mountain
shān-míng shuǐ-xiù	山明水秀	green hills and clear waters
shān xià	山下	at the foot of a hill or mountain
shang		
shāngdiàn	商店	shop
shàng	上	up, upper, upward
shàng kè	上课	have class, attend class
shàngwǔ	上午	morning
shao		
shǎo	少	few, little, less

74

shàonián	少年	early youth, juvenile
she		
shétou	舌头	tongue
shéhuì	社会	society
shei		
shéi	谁	who
shéide	谁的	whose
shéi lái	谁来	who will come
shéi qù	谁去	who will go
shéi tīng	谁听	who will listen to ...
shéi zǒu	谁走	who will leave
shen		
shēn-qiáng tǐ-zhuàng	身强体壮	(of a person) strong and sturdy
shēnti	身体	body, health
shénme	什么	what
shènzhòng	慎重	cautious, prudent
sheng		
shēng	生	give birth to, bear, grow, get
shēngbìng	生病	fall ill, get ill
shēngchǎn	生产	produce, manufacture
shēngrì	生日	birthday
shènglì	胜利	win, victory
shi		
shí	十	ten
shíhou	时候	time, moment
shíjiān	时间	time, all the days of the past, present and future

shísì	十四	fourteen
shítáng	食堂	dining hall
shítou	石头	stone, rock
shíyuè	十月	October
shìr	事儿	matter, thing, affair, business
shì yī shì	试一试	have a try
shì	是	be
shou		
shǒu	手	hand
shǒubiǎo	手表	wrist-watch
shǒudū	首都	capital (of a country)
shòuhuòyuán	售货员	salesclerk
shu		
shū	书	book
shūbāo	书包	satchel, schoolbag
shūfu	舒服	comfortable
shūshu	叔叔	father's younger brother, uncle
shǔ	数	to count, to reckon
shùr	数儿	number, figure
shù	树	tree
shùyè	树叶	leaf
shuai		
shuāi	摔	fall, tumble
shuāi huài	摔坏	to fall off and get broken
shui		
shui	水	water, liquid

shuǐguǒ	水果	fruit
shuo		
shuō	说	speak, talk, say
shuōle yòu shuō	说了又说	explain and explain again, to keep talking
shuō Zhōngguóhuà	说中国话	speak Chinese
si		
sījī	司机	driver
sīxiǎng	思想	idea, thought, thinking,
sì	四	four
sìshí	四十	forty
song		
sòng	送	deliver, carry, give as a present
sònggěi	送给	send sth. to sb.
su		
sùshè	宿舍	dormitory, hostel
sui		
suì	岁	years of age

T

ta		
tā*	他(她)	he (or she)
tā bú qù	他不去	he won't go
tāde	他的	his
tā huǒrle	他火儿了	he flared up

---

*"她", a personal pronoun, is sounded exactly the same as "他". In writing, "他" is used to denote a male person while "她" a female one.

tā jǐ suì	他几岁	how old is he
tā lái	他来	he will come
tāmen	他们	they
tā qù	他去	he will leave
tā ne	他呢	what (how) about him
tā shì shéi	他是谁	who is he
tā tīng	他听	he will listen
tā zǒu	他走	he will go

tai

tài*	太	too, over, excessively
táidēng	台灯	desk lamp, table lamp
tài cháng	太长	too long
tài gāo	太高	too high, too tall
tài jìn	太近	too close
tàiyáng	太阳	the sun
tài yuǎn	太远	too far

tan

| tānkāi | 摊开 | spread sth. out |
| tàntǎo | 探讨 | inquire into, probe into |

tang

tāng	汤	soup, broth
táng	糖	sugar, sweets
tǎng	躺	lie, recline
tàng	烫	scald, very hot

---

*Adverb "太" usually means "excessively", "too" or "over". But when it appears in an exclamatory sentence, it represents only an emphatic "very", e.g. "太好了！" (very good!)

te

tèbié	特别	special, particular extra-ordinary

ti

tī	踢	kick
tī qíu	踢球	play football
tíxǐng	提醒	remind, warn
tíyù	体育	physical culture

tian

tiān	天	sky, heaven
tiānqì	天气	weather
tiān shang	天上	in the sky
tián biǎo	填表	fill in a form

tiao

tiào	跳	jump, leap
tiàowǔ	跳舞	dance

tie

tiē	贴	paste, stick
tiēqiè	贴切	apt, suitable

ting

tīng	听	listen, hear
tīng dǒngle	听懂了	have understood
tíngzhǐ	停止	stop, halt

tong

tóngděng	同等	of the same class (rank or status), on an equal basis
tóngzhì	同志	comrade
tōngzhī	通知	notify, give notice

tu

| túdì | 徒弟 | apprentice, disciple |
| túhuà | 图画 | drawing, picture |

W

wai

wài	外	outer, outward, outside
wàiguó	外国	foreign country
wàijiāobù	外交部	the Ministry of Foreign Affairs

wan

wánr	玩	play, have fun
wǎnfàn	晚饭	supper, dinner
wǎnshang	晚上	evening, at night
wàn-gǔ líu-fāng	万古流芳	leave a good reputation which will go down to posterity

wei

wèile	为了	for, so as to
wèi shénme	为什么	why
wèishēng	卫生	hygiene

wen

wēndù	温度	temperature
wēnnuǎn	温暖	warm
wèn	问	ask, inquire
wèntí	问题	question, problem
wénhuà	文化	civilization, culture
wénwù	文物	cultural relic

wo

wǒ	我	I, me
wǒ chī	我吃	I eat, have my meal
wǒde	我的	my, mine
wǒde shū	我的书	my book
wǒ kàn	我看	I'll have a look
wǒ lái	我来	I'll come
wǒ mǎi mǐ	我买米	I'll buy some rice
wǒ mǎi mì	我买蜜	I'll buy some honey
wǒmen	我们	we
wǒ qù	我去	I'll go
wǒ tīng	我听	I'll listen
wǒ zǒu	我走	I'll leave

wu

wūzi	屋子	room
wǔ	五	five
wǔtái	舞台	stage, arena

X

xi

xī	西	west
xībiān	西边	west side
xíguàn	习惯	habits, be used to
xǐhuan	喜欢	like, enjoy
xǐzǎo	洗澡	take a bath

xia

xià	下	below, down, under, lower, next, latter

81

xià kè	下课	finish class, the class is over
xiàlai	下来	come down
xiàqu	下去	go down, go on
xiàtiān	夏天	summer
xiàwǔ	下午	afternoon
xià xuě	下雪	snow is falling, it's snowing
xià xīngqī	下星期	next week
xià yǔ	下雨	rain is falling, it's raining

xian

xiān	先	earlier, befor, first
xiānhuā	鲜花	fresh flowers
xiānsheng	先生	teacher, mister, gentle-man
xiànmù	羡慕	admire, envy
xiànzài	现在	now, at present
xiān zǒu	先走	go first

xiang

xiāng	香	fragrant, aromatic, scent-ed, sweet-smelling
xiānghuā	香花	fragrant flower, sweet flower
xiāngzi	箱子	chest, trunk, box, case
xiǎng	想	think, suppose
xiǎngdào	想到	to think of, to call to mind
xiǎngliàng	响亮	loud and clear
xiǎng tīng	想听	want to listen (to sth.)

xiàngqián	向前	go forward
xiao		
xiāoxi	消息	news, message
xiǎo	小	small, little, minor
xiǎo dāo	小刀	small sword, pocket knife
xiǎoháir	小孩儿	child
xiǎoniǎo	小鸟	bird
xiǎo qíu	小球	a small ball
xiǎoshuō	小说	novel, fiction
xiào	笑	smile, laugh
xiàohua	笑话	joke, jest
xiàozhǎng	校长	chancellor, president
xiàozhe shuō	笑着说	say sth. in smile
xie		
xiě xìn	写信	write a letter
xièxie	谢谢	thanks
xìn		
xīn	心	the heart, mind
xīn-míng yǎn-liàng	心明眼亮	be sharp-eyed and clear-headed
xīn	新	new, fresh
xīnnián	新年	New Year
xīnqíng	心情	mood, frame (or state) of mind
xīnwén	新闻	news
xīnxian	新鲜	fresh, new
xìn	信	letter, mail
xìnfēng	信封	envelope

xing

xíng	行	all right
xíng bu xíng	行不行	is it right, is it O.K.
xìng	姓	surname, family (or clan) name
xìng shénme	姓什么	what's your (his etc.) surname

xiong

xiōng	胸	chest, bosom
xiōngdì	兄弟	brothers
xiōngyǒng	汹涌	tempestuous, turbulent
xiōngzhāng	胸章	badge

xiu

xiū	修	repair, mend
xiūxi	休息	rest, have a rest

xu

xūyào	需要	need, want

xuan

xuǎn	选	pick, elect, select
xuǎnzé	选择	select, choose

xue

xué	学	study, learn
xué hǎo	学好	emulate good
xuéxí	学习	study, learn, emulate
xuéyuàn	学院	college, institute

xun

xūnzhāng	勋章	medal, decoration

Y

yan

yánsè	颜色	colour
yǎnjing	眼睛	eye
yǎnyuán	演员	actor, actress

yang

yángguāng	阳光	sunlight, sunshine
yàngzi	样子	appearance, shape

yao

yào	要	want to, wish to
yàoshì	要是	if, suppose, in case
yào-wǔ yáng-wēi	耀武扬威	make a show of one's strength
yào zhème shuō	要这么说	say it this way

ye

yéye	爷爷	grandfather, grandpa
yě	也	also, too
yèli	夜里	at night

yi

yī*	一	a, one
yìbǎ	一把	a handful of ...
yíbiàn	一遍	one time
yíbànr	一半儿	one half
yídùn fàn	一顿饭	a (one) meal

---

*"一" is pronounced in the 1st tone (yī) when it stands by itself, but is pronounced in the 4th tone (yì) when it precedes a 1st, 2nd or 3rd tone, and is pronounced in the 2nd tone (yí) when it precedes a 4th tone.

yíge rén	一个人	a man, a single person
yígòng	一共	altogether, in all
yíhuìr	一会儿	a moment, a little while
yí kuài	一块	a piece of ...
yí kuàir	一块儿	together
yìbiānr	一边儿	one side, at the same time
yìdiǎnr	一点儿	a bit, a little
yìzhí	一直	always, all along
yīfu	衣服	clothes
yīshēng	医生	doctor
yǐhòu	以后	after, afterwards
yǐjīng	已经	already
yǐqián	以前	before, formerly
yǐwéi	以为	think, believe, consider
yǐzi	椅子	chair
yin		
yīnwéi	因为	because
yīnyuè	音乐	music
yínháng	银行	bank
ying		
yīngyǔ	英语	English
yong		
yǒngyuǎn	永远	forever, always
yòng	用	use
yòng shénme	用什么	what do you make use of
yòng shǒu	用手	use one's hands
yòng nǎo	用脑	use one's head

yòng yǎn	用眼	use one's own eyes
yòng shuǐ	用水	use water
you		
yōuměi	优美	beautiful, graceful
yóujú	邮局	post office
yóuyǒng	游泳	swim, swimming
yǒu*	有	have, there is (are)
yǒu bǎwò	有把握	be sure that, to have great certainty of
yǒu qián	有钱	have money, to be rich
yǒu diǎnr	有点儿	somewhat, rather a bit
yǒu rén zhǎo nǐ	有人找你	someone is looking for you
yǒu shénme shìr	有什么事儿	what business have you here
yǒuyòng	有用	be useful
yǒuhǎo	友好	close friend, friendly
yǒuyì	友谊	friendship
yòu kuài yòu hǎo	又快又好	fast and well
yu		
yúkuài	愉快	happy, merry
yǔjù	语句	sentence
yǔyán	语言	language
yǔyī	雨衣	raincoat, waterproof
yùdào	遇到	run into, come across

---

*The negative form of "有" in the sentence is made by putting the adverb "没" (měi) instead of "不" (bù) in front of the verb "有".

yuánlái	原来	original, former, originally
yuánliàng	原谅	excuse, pardon
yuànyì	愿意	want, wish, willing to
yun		
yùn	运	carry, transport
yuèliang	月亮	the moon
yuēlüè	约略	roughly, approximate

Z

za		
zá	杂	mixed, sundry
zázhì	杂志	magazine
zai		
zài	在	at, in, exist
zài	再	again, once more
zàijiàn	再见	goodbye
zàisān	再三	again and again
zài lǐmian	在里面	inside
zài zhèr	在这儿	here
zài zuò	再做	do it again
zan		
zánmen	咱们	we (inclusive of first person)
zao		
zǎo	早	early, long ago
zǎoshang	早上	(early) morning
zǎocāo	早操	morning exercises

zen

zěnme	怎么	what, why, how
zěnmeyàng	怎么样	what, how

zhan

zhànchǎng	战场	battle front

zhang

zhǎng	长	grow
zhǎngde cháng	长得长	grow longer
zhǎngde gāo	长得高	grow taller

zhao

zháojí	着急	worry, feel anxious
zháo huǒ	着火	catch fire, be on fire
zhǎo	找	look for, try to find, seek
zhǎo ge zuòr	找个座儿	try to look for a seat
zhǎo shénme	找什么	what are you looking for
zhàoxiàng	照相	take a photo

zhe

zhè	这	this
zhèhuìr	这会儿	at the moment
zhè jiàn shì	这件事	this thing, this business
zhème	这么	so, such, this way
zhèr	这儿	here
zhèshì	这是	this is
zhè xie	这些	these

zhen

zhēn	真	true, real, truly, indeed
zhēn cháng	真长	be really long
zhēn gāo	真高	be truly tall

zhēn jìn	真近	be really close
zhēn liángkuài	真凉快	it's pleasantly cool
zhēn yuǎn	真远	be really far
zhēnzhèng	真正	genuine, real, true
zhēn zhǔn	真准	it's accurate
zhěntóu	枕头	pillow
zheng		
zhěng	整	whole, full
zhěngjié	整洁	clean and neat, spick and span
zhěngqí	整齐	in good order, neat and tidy
zhèng	正	straight, upright
zhèngcháng	正常	normal, regular
zhèngfǔ	政府	government
zhènghǎo	正好	suitable, fit, just
zhi		
zhīdào	知道	know, realize
zhīshi	知识	knowledge
zhǐshì	指示	instruct, instruction
zhǐyǒu	只有	only by, only in this way
zhong		
zhōng	中	centre, middle
Zhōngguó	中国	China
zhōngjiān	中间	middle
zhǒngzhǒng	种种	all kinds of
zhòng	种	grow, plant
zhu		
zhǔrén	主人	owner, host, master

zhǔrèn	主任	director, head
zhùhè	祝贺	congratulate, congratulation
zhù	住	live, stay, reside
zhù zai nǎr	住在哪	where does . . . live
zhuan		
zhuǎn	转	turn, shift
zhuǎnhuàn	转换	change, transform
zi		
zixì kàn	仔细看	look at it carefully
zìjǐ	自己	oneself
zìsī	自私	selfish
zou		
zǒu	走	walk, go
zǒu ba	走吧	let's go
zǒu yi zǒu	走一走	take a walk
zui		
zui	嘴	mouth
zuì	最	most
zuìhǎo	最好	best of all, had better
zuo		
zuótiān	昨天	yesterday
zuǒ	左	left
zuǒbiān	左边	the left side
zuǒ-yòu shǒu	左右手	right-hand man
zuò cāo	作操	do gymnastics, do exercises
zuò	坐	sit

zuò fēijī	坐飞机	by aeroplane
zuòwèi	座位	seat, a place to sit
zuò xià	坐下	sit down
zuòyè	作业	homework, assignment

中国话听力（一）

中国话语音基础

*

外文出版社出版
（中国北京百万庄路24号）
外文印刷厂印刷
中国国际书店发行
（北京399信箱）
1983年（40开）第一版
编号：（英汉）9050—54
00090
9—E—1691P